Contents

Roast Tomato-Basil Soup

2 cans (28 ounces each) peeled whole tomatoes, drained and liquid reserved

21/2 tablespoons packed dark brown sugar

1 medium onion, finely chopped

3 cups tomato liquid reserved from canned tomatoes

3 cups chicken broth

3 tablespoons tomato paste

1/4 teaspoon ground allspice

1 can (5 ounces) evaporated milk

1/4 cup shredded fresh basil leaves (about 10 large)

Salt and black pepper

1. Preheat oven to 450°F. Line baking sheet with foil; spray with nonstick cooking spray. Arrange tomatoes on foil in single layer. Sprinkle with brown sugar and top with onion. Bake about 25 to 30 minutes or until tomatoes look dry and light brown. Let tomatoes cool slightly; finely chop.

2. Place tomato mixture, 3 cups reserved liquid from canned tomatoes, chicken broth, tomato paste and allspice in slow cooker. Mix well. Cover; cook on LOW 8 hours or on HIGH 4 hours.

3. Add evaporated milk and basil; season with salt and pepper. Cook on HIGH 30 minutes or until hot. Garnish as desired. 	*Makes 6 servings*

Easy Corn Chowder

2 cans (14½ ounces each) chicken broth
1 bag (16 ounces) frozen corn kernels
3 small potatoes, peeled and cut into ½-inch pieces
1 red bell pepper, diced
1 medium onion, diced
1 rib celery, sliced
½ teaspoon salt
½ teaspoon black pepper
¼ teaspoon ground coriander
½ cup heavy cream
8 slices bacon, crisp-cooked and crumbled

1. Place broth, corn, potatoes, bell pepper, onion, celery, salt, black pepper and coriander into slow cooker. Cover; cook on LOW 7 to 8 hours.

2. Partially mash soup mixture with potato masher to thicken. Stir in cream; cook on HIGH, uncovered, until hot. Adjust seasonings, if desired. Garnish with bacon.   *Makes 6 servings*

Chicken Stew

4 to 5 cups chopped cooked chicken (about 5 boneless skinless chicken breasts)
1 can (28 ounces) whole tomatoes, undrained
2 large potatoes, cut into 1-inch pieces
½ pound okra, sliced
1 large onion, chopped
1 can (14 ounces) cream-style corn
½ cup ketchup
½ cup barbecue sauce

1. Combine chicken, tomatoes with juice, potatoes, okra and onion in slow cooker. Cover; cook on LOW 6 to 8 hours or until potatoes are tender.

2. Add corn, ketchup and barbecue sauce. Cover; cook on HIGH 30 minutes.   *Makes 6 servings*

Serving Suggestion: Serve this stew with hot crusty rolls and a green salad to complete your meal.

Navy Bean & Ham Soup

6 cups water
5 cups dried navy beans, soaked overnight and drained
1 pound ham, cubed
1 can (15 ounces) corn, drained
1 can (4 ounces) mild diced green chilies, drained
1 onion, diced (optional)
   Salt and black pepper to taste

Place all ingredients in slow cooker. Cover; cook on LOW 8 to 10 hours or until beans are tender. *Makes 6 servings.*

Serving Suggestion: Serve with freshly baked biscuits.

Three-Bean Turkey Chili

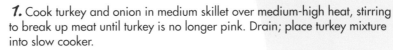

1 **pound ground turkey**
1 **small onion, chopped**
1 **can (28 ounces) diced tomatoes, undrained**
1 **can (15 ounces) chick-peas (garbanzo beans), rinsed and drained**
1 **can (15 ounces) kidney beans, rinsed and drained**
1 **can (15 ounces) black beans, rinsed and drained**
1 **can (8 ounces) tomato sauce**
1 **can (about 4 ounces) chopped mild green chilies**
1 **to 2 tablespoons chili powder**

1. Cook turkey and onion in medium skillet over medium-high heat, stirring to break up meat until turkey is no longer pink. Drain; place turkey mixture into slow cooker.

2. Add remaining ingredients and mix well. Cover; cook on HIGH 6 to 8 hours. *Makes 6 to 8 servings*

Country Chicken Chowder

2 tablespoons butter or margarine
1½ pounds chicken tenders, cut into ½-inch pieces
2 small onions, chopped
2 ribs celery, sliced
2 small carrots, sliced
2 cups frozen corn
2 cans (10¾ ounces each) cream of potato soup, undiluted
1½ cups chicken broth
1 teaspoon dried dill weed
½ cup half-and-half

1. Melt butter in large skillet. Add chicken; cook until browned. Add cooked chicken, onions, celery, carrots, corn, soup, chicken broth and dill to slow cooker. Cover and cook on LOW 3 to 4 hours or until chicken is no longer pink and vegetables are tender.

2. Turn off heat; stir in half-and-half. Cover and let stand 5 to 10 minutes or just until heated through. *Makes 8 servings*

Note: For a special touch, garnish soup with croutons and fresh dill.

Simple Turkey Soup

2 pounds ground turkey, cooked and drained
1 can (28 ounces) whole tomatoes, undrained
2 cans (14 ounces each) beef broth
1 bag (16 ounces) frozen mixed soup vegetables (such as carrots,
beans, okra, corn or onion)
½ cup uncooked barley
1 teaspoon salt
1 teaspoon dried thyme leaves
½ teaspoon ground coriander
Black pepper

Combine all ingredients in slow cooker. Add water to cover. Cover; cook on
HIGH 3 to 4 hours or until barley and vegetables are tender.

Makes 8 servings

Serving Suggestion: Serve this soup with cornbread.

Chunky Chili

1 pound 90% lean ground beef
1 medium onion, chopped
1 tablespoon chili powder
1½ teaspoons ground cumin
  2 cans (16 ounces each) diced tomatoes, undrained
  1 can (15 ounces) pinto beans, rinsed and drained
  ½ cup prepared salsa
  ½ cup (2 ounces) shredded Cheddar cheese
  ¼ cup diced onions
  4 teaspoons sliced black olives

Heat large skillet over medium heat. Add beef and onion, cook until beef is browned and onion is tender. Drain fat. Place beef mixture, chili powder, tomatoes, beans and salsa in slow cooker; stir. Cover; cook on LOW 5 to 6 hours or until flavors are blended and chili is bubbly. Season with salt and pepper to taste. Serve with cheese, onions and olives.

Makes 4 (1½-cup) servings

Serving Suggestion: Serve with tossed green salad and cornbread muffins.

Winter's Best Bean Soup

6 ounces bacon, diced
10 cups chicken broth
3 cans (15 ounces each) Great Northern beans, drained
1 can (14½ ounces) diced tomatoes, undrained
1 large onion, chopped
1 package (10 ounces) frozen sliced or diced carrots
2 teaspoons bottled minced garlic
1 fresh rosemary sprig *or* 1 teaspoon dried rosemary
1 teaspoon black pepper

1. Cook bacon in medium skillet over medium-high heat until just cooked; drain and transfer to slow cooker. Add remaining ingredients.

2. Cover; cook on LOW 8 hours or until beans are tender. Remove rosemary sprig and mince the leaves before serving.

Makes 8 to 10 servings

Serving Suggestion: Place slices of toasted Italian bread in bottom of individual soup bowls. Drizzle with olive oil. Pour soup over bread and serve.

Slow Cooker Chicken & Rice

3 cans (10¾ ounces each) condensed cream of chicken soup, undiluted
2 cups uncooked instant rice
1 cup water
1 pound boneless skinless chicken breasts or chicken breast tenders
½ teaspoon salt
¼ teaspoon black pepper
¼ teaspoon paprika
½ cup diced celery

Combine soup, rice and water in slow cooker. Add chicken; sprinkle with salt, pepper and paprika. Sprinkle celery over chicken. Cover; cook on LOW 6 to 8 hours or on HIGH 3 to 4 hours.   *Makes 4 servings*

savory chicken   13

Italian Chicken with Sausage and Peppers

2½ pounds chicken pieces
2 tablespoons olive oil
½ to ¾ pounds sweet Italian sausage
2 green bell peppers, chopped
1 onion, chopped
1 carrot, finely chopped
2 cloves garlic, minced
1 can (15 ounces) tomato sauce
1 can (19 ounces) condensed tomato soup, undiluted
¼ teaspoon dried oregano
¼ teaspoon dried basil
1 bay leaf
Salt and pepper

1. Rinse chicken; pat dry. Heat oil in large skillet over medium-high heat. Add chicken, skin side down. Cook about 10 minutes, turning to brown both sides. Remove and reserve.

2. Add sausage to skillet and cook 4 to 5 minutes or until browned. Remove and cut into 1-inch pieces; reserve. Drain off all but 1 tablespoon fat from skillet.

3. Add bell peppers, onion, carrot and garlic to skillet. Cook 4 to 5 minutes or until vegetables are tender.

4. Add tomato sauce, tomato soup, oregano, basil and bay leaf; stir well. Season with salt and pepper. Transfer to slow cooker.

5. Add chicken and sausage to slow cooker. Cover; cook on LOW 6 to 8 hours or on HIGH 4 to 6 hours. Remove and discard bay leaf before serving.

Makes 6 servings

Easy Parmesan Chicken

8 ounces fresh mushrooms, sliced
1 medium onion, cut into thin wedges
1 tablespoon olive oil
4 boneless skinless chicken breasts
1 jar (26 ounces) pasta sauce
½ teaspoon dried basil leaves
¼ teaspoon dried oregano leaves
1 bay leaf
½ cup (2 ounces) shredded part-skim mozzarella cheese
¼ cup grated Parmesan cheese
   Hot cooked spaghetti

1. Place mushrooms and onion in slow cooker.

2. Heat oil in large skillet over medium-high heat until hot. Lightly brown chicken on both sides. Place chicken in slow cooker. Pour pasta sauce over chicken; add herbs. Cover; cook on LOW 6 to 7 hours or on HIGH 3 hours or until chicken is no longer pink in center. Remove and discard bay leaf.

3. Sprinkle chicken with cheeses. Cook, uncovered, on LOW 15 to 30 minutes or until cheeses are melted. Serve over spaghetti.

Makes 4 servings

Serving Suggestion: Other vegetables, such as sliced zucchini, cubed eggplant or broccoli florets, can be substituted for the mushroom slices.

Savory chicken

Mile-High Enchilada Pie

8 (6-inch) corn tortillas
1 jar (12 ounces) prepared salsa
1 can (15½ ounces) kidney beans, rinsed and drained
1 cup shredded cooked chicken
1 cup shredded Monterey Jack cheese with jalapeño peppers

Prepare foil handles for slow cooker (see below); place in slow cooker. Place 1 tortilla on bottom of slow cooker. Top with small amount of salsa, beans, chicken and cheese. Continue layering using remaining ingredients, ending with cheese. Cover; cook on LOW 6 to 8 hours or on HIGH 3 to 4 hours. Pull out by foil handles. Garnish with fresh cilantro and slice of red bell pepper, if desired. *Makes 4 to 6 servings*

Foil Handles: Tear off three 18×2-inch strips of heavy foil or use regular foil folded to double thickness. Crisscross foil strips in spoke design and place in slow cooker to make lifting of tortilla stack easier.

Chicken Parisienne

6 boneless skinless chicken breasts (about 1½ pounds), cubed
½ teaspoon salt
½ teaspoon black pepper
½ teaspoon paprika
1 can (10¾ ounces) condensed cream of mushroom or cream of
**   chicken soup, undiluted**
2 cans (4 ounces each) sliced mushrooms, drained
½ cup dry white wine
1 cup sour cream
6 cups hot cooked egg noodles

1. Place chicken in slow cooker. Sprinkle with salt, pepper and paprika. Add soup, mushrooms and wine to slow cooker; mix well.

2. Cover; cook on HIGH 2 to 3 hours.

3. Add sour cream during last 30 minutes of cooking. Serve over noodles. Garnish as desired.   *Makes 6 servings*

Serving Suggestion: For a taste-pleasing variation, try this dish over rice instead of noodles.

Kat's Slow Chicken

4 to 6 boneless skinless breasts *or* 1 cut-up whole chicken (3 pounds)
1 jar (26 ounces) pasta sauce
1 medium onion, sliced
1 medium green bell pepper, cut into strips
4 carrots, sliced
1 rib celery, sliced
4 cloves garlic, minced
½ teaspoon salt
2 tablespoons to ¼ cup water, divided
1 to 2 tablespoons cornstarch
Prepared mashed potatoes or hot cooked noodles (optional)

Combine all ingredients, except water, cornstarch and mashed potatoes in slow cooker. Cover; cook on LOW 6 to 8 hours. Before serving, combine 2 tablespoons water and 1 tablespoon cornstarch in small bowl. Stir until mixture is smooth. Add to slow cooker. Cook on HIGH an additional 15 minutes or until mixture thickens. If mixture needs additional thickening, add remaining water and cornstarch. Serve chicken and vegetables over mashed potatoes, if desired.   *Makes 4 servings*

Savory Chicken

Old World Chicken and Vegetables

1 tablespoon dried oregano leaves
1 teaspoon salt, divided
1 teaspoon paprika
½ teaspoon garlic powder
¼ teaspoon black pepper
2 medium green bell peppers, cut into thin strips
1 small yellow onion, thinly sliced
1 cut-up whole chicken (3 pounds)
⅓ cup ketchup
6 ounces uncooked egg noodles

1. Combine oregano, ½ teaspoon salt, paprika, garlic powder and black pepper in small bowl; mix well.

2. Place bell peppers and onion in slow cooker. Top with chicken thighs and legs, sprinkle with half the oregano mixture, top with chicken breasts. Sprinkle chicken with remaining oregano mixture. Cover; cook on LOW 8 hours or on HIGH 4 hours. Stir in ketchup and remaining ½ teaspoon salt.

3. Just before serving, cook noodles following package directions; drain. Serve chicken and vegetables over noodles.   *Makes 4 servings*

Chicken with Italian Sausage

10 ounces bulk mild or hot Italian sausage
6 boneless skinless chicken thighs
1 can (about 15 ounces) Great Northern beans, rinsed and
    drained
1 can (about 15 ounces) kidney beans, rinsed and drained
1 cup chicken broth
1 medium onion, chopped
1 teaspoon black pepper
½ teaspoon salt
    Chopped fresh parsley

1. Brown sausage in large skillet over medium-high heat, stirring to separate; drain fat. Spoon into slow cooker.

2. Trim fat from chicken. Place chicken, beans, broth, onion, pepper and salt in slow cooker. Cover; cook on LOW 5 to 6 hours.

3. Adjust seasonings, if desired. Slice each chicken thigh on the diagonal. Serve with sausage and beans. Garnish with parsley, if desired.

Makes 6 servings

Turkey and Macaroni

1 teaspoon vegetable oil
1½ pounds ground turkey
2 cans (10¾ ounces each) condensed tomato soup, undiluted
2 cups uncooked macaroni
1 can (16 ounces) corn, drained
½ cup chopped onion
1 can (4 ounces) sliced mushrooms, drained
2 tablespoons ketchup
1 tablespoon mustard
Salt and black pepper to taste

1. Heat oil in medium skillet; cook turkey until browned. Transfer turkey to slow cooker.

2. Add soup, macaroni, corn, onion, mushrooms, ketchup, mustard, salt and pepper to slow cooker. Stir to blend.

3. Cover; cook on LOW 7 to 9 hours or on HIGH 3 to 4 hours.

Makes 4 to 6 servings

Turkey Meatballs in Cranberry-Barbecue Sauce

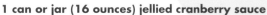

1 can or jar (16 ounces) jellied cranberry sauce
½ cup barbecue sauce
1 egg white
1 pound 93% lean ground turkey
1 green onion with top, sliced
2 teaspoons grated orange peel
1 teaspoon reduced-sodium soy sauce
¼ teaspoon black pepper
⅛ teaspoon ground red pepper (optional)

1. Combine cranberry sauce and barbecue sauce in slow cooker. Cover; cook on HIGH 20 to 30 minutes or until cranberry sauce is melted and mixture is hot.

2. Meanwhile, place egg white in medium bowl; beat lightly. Add turkey, green onion, orange peel, soy sauce, black pepper and ground red pepper, if desired; mix well with hands until well blended. Shape into 24 balls.

3. Spray large nonstick skillet with nonstick cooking spray. Add meatballs to skillet; cook over medium heat 8 to 10 minutes or until meatballs are no longer pink in center, carefully turning occasionally to brown evenly. Add to heated sauce in slow cooker; stir gently to coat.

4. Reduce heat to LOW. Cover; cook 3 hours. Transfer meatballs to serving plate; garnish, if desired. Serve with decorative picks.

Makes 12 servings

Saucy Tropical Turkey

3 to 4 turkey thighs, skin removed (about 2½ pounds)
2 tablespoons cooking oil
1 small onion, halved and sliced
1 can (20 ounces) pineapple chunks, drained
1 red bell pepper, cubed
⅔ cup apricot preserves
3 tablespoons soy sauce
1 teaspoon grated lemon peel
1 teaspoon ground ginger
¼ cup cold water
2 tablespoons cornstarch
Hot cooked rice or noodles

1. Rinse turkey and pat dry. Heat oil in large skillet; brown turkey on all sides. Place onion in slow cooker. Transfer turkey to slow cooker and top with pineapple and bell pepper.

2. Combine preserves, soy sauce, lemon peel and ginger in small bowl; mix well. Spoon over turkey. Cover; cook on LOW 6 to 7 hours.

3. Remove turkey from slow cooker; keep warm. Blend water and cornstarch until smooth; stir into slow cooker. Cook on HIGH 15 minutes or until sauce is slightly thickened. Adjust seasonings, if desired. Return turkey to slow cooker; cook until hot. Serve with rice.   *Makes 6 servings*

Tasty Turkey

Turkey Tacos

1 pound ground turkey
1 medium onion, chopped
1 can (6 ounces) tomato paste
½ cup chunky salsa
1 tablespoon chopped fresh cilantro
¾ teaspoon salt, divided
1 tablespoon butter
1 tablespoon all-purpose flour
⅓ cup milk
½ cup sour cream
Ground red pepper
8 taco shells

1. Brown turkey and onion in large skillet over medium heat, stirring to separate meat. Combine turkey mixture, tomato paste, salsa, cilantro and ½ teaspoon salt in slow cooker. Cover; cook on LOW 4 to 5 hours.

2. Just before serving, melt butter in small saucepan over low heat. Stir in flour and remaining ¼ teaspoon salt; cook 1 minute. Carefully stir in milk. Cook and stir over low heat until thickened. Remove from heat. Combine sour cream and dash ground red pepper in small bowl. Stir into hot milk mixture. Return to heat; cook over low heat 1 minute, stirring constantly.

3. Spoon ¼ cup turkey mixture into each taco shell; keep warm. Spoon sour cream mixture over taco filling.　　　　　　　*Makes 8 tacos*

Tasty Turkey

Slow Cooker Stuffed Peppers

1 package (about 7 ounces) Spanish rice mix
1 pound ground beef
½ cup diced celery
1 small onion, chopped
1 egg, beaten
4 medium green bell peppers, halved lengthwise, cored and seeded
1 can (28 ounces) whole peeled tomatoes, undrained
1 can (10¾ ounces) condensed tomato soup, undiluted
1 cup water

1. Set aside seasoning packet from rice. Combine beef, rice mix, celery, onion and egg in large bowl. Divide meat mixture evenly among pepper halves.

2. Pour tomatoes with juice into slow cooker. Arrange filled pepper halves on top of tomatoes. Combine tomato soup, water and reserved rice mix seasoning packet in medium bowl. Pour over peppers. Cover; cook on LOW 8 to 10 hours.   *Makes 4 servings*

Beef with Apples and Sweet Potatoes

1 boneless beef chuck shoulder roast (2 pounds)
1 can (40 ounces) sweet potatoes, drained
2 small onions, sliced
2 apples, cored and sliced
½ cup beef broth
2 cloves garlic, minced
1 teaspoon salt
1 teaspoon dried thyme leaves, divided
¾ teaspoon black pepper, divided
1 tablespoon cornstarch
¼ teaspoon ground cinnamon
2 tablespoons cold water

1. Trim fat from beef and cut into 2-inch pieces. Place beef, sweet potatoes, onions, apples, beef broth, garlic, salt, ½ teaspoon thyme and ½ teaspoon pepper in slow cooker. Cover; cook on LOW 8 to 9 hours.

2. Transfer beef, sweet potatoes and apples to platter; keep warm. Let liquid stand 5 minutes to allow fat to rise. Skim off fat.

3. Combine cornstarch, remaining ½ teaspoon thyme, ¼ teaspoon pepper, cinnamon and water; stir into cooking liquid. Cook 15 minutes or until juices are thickened. Serve sauce with beef, sweet potatoes and apples.

Makes 6 servings

Slow Cooker Pizza Casserole

4 jars (14 ounces each) pizza sauce
1½ pounds ground beef, cooked and drained
1 pound sausage, cooked and drained
1 pound corkscrew pasta, cooked and drained
2 cups (8 ounces) shredded mozzarella cheese
2 cups freshly grated Parmesan cheese
2 cans (4 ounces each) mushroom stems and pieces, drained
2 packages (3 ounces each) sliced pepperoni
½ cup finely chopped onion
½ cup finely chopped green bell pepper
1 clove garlic, minced

1. Combine all ingredients in slow cooker.

2. Cover; cook on LOW 4 hours or on HIGH 2 hours.

Makes 6 servings

Beef Dishes

Mexican Meatloaf

2 pounds ground beef
2 cups crushed corn or tortilla chips
1 cup shredded Cheddar cheese
⅔ cup salsa
2 eggs, beaten
4 tablespoons taco seasoning

1. Combine all ingredients in large bowl; mix well.

2. Shape meat mixture into loaf and place in slow cooker. Cover; cook on LOW 8 to 10 hours.   *Makes 4 to 6 servings*

Tip: For a glaze, mix together ½ cup ketchup, 2 tablespoons brown sugar and 1 teaspoon dry mustard. Spread over meatloaf. Cover; cook on HIGH 15 minutes.

Sloppy Sloppy Joes

4 pounds ground beef
1 cup chopped onion
1 cup chopped green bell pepper
1 can (about 28 ounces) tomato sauce
2 cans (10¾ ounces each) condensed tomato soup, undiluted
1 cup packed brown sugar
¼ cup ketchup
3 tablespoons Worcestershire sauce
1 tablespoon dry mustard
1 tablespoon prepared mustard
1½ teaspoons chili powder
1 teaspoon garlic powder

1. Cook beef in large skillet over medium-high heat until no longer pink, stirring to break up meat. Drain fat. Add onion and green pepper and cook, stirring frequently, 5 to 10 minutes or until onion becomes translucent and mixture becomes fragrant.

2. Transfer meat mixture to slow cooker. Add remaining ingredients; stir well to combine.

3. Cover; cook on LOW 4 to 6 hours.   *Makes 20 to 25 servings*

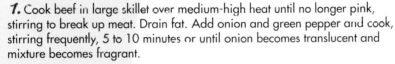

Harvest Ham Supper

6 carrots, sliced in half lengthwise
3 sweet potatoes, sliced in half lengthwise
1½ pounds boneless ham
1 cup maple syrup

1. Place carrots and potatoes in bottom of slow cooker to form a rack. Place ham on top of vegetables. Pour syrup over ham and vegetables.

2. Cover; cook on LOW 6 to 8 hours.

Makes 6 servings

Maple Syrup

Simply Delicious Pork

1½ **pounds boneless pork loin, cut into 6 pieces or 6 boneless pork loin chops**
4 **medium Yellow Delicious apples, sliced**
3 **tablespoons brown sugar**
1 **teaspoon ground cinnamon**
½ **teaspoon salt**

1. Place pork in slow cooker. Cover with apples.

2. Combine brown sugar, cinnamon and salt in small bowl; sprinkle over apples. Cover; cook on LOW 6 to 8 hours.   *Makes 6 servings*

Peachy Pork

2 cans (about 15 ounces each) sliced peaches in heavy syrup, undrained
6 to 8 boneless pork blade or top loin chops (about 2 pounds)
1 small onion, thinly sliced
½ cup golden raisins
¼ cup packed light brown sugar
3 tablespoons cider vinegar
2 tablespoons tapioca
1 teaspoon salt
¾ teaspoon ground cinnamon
¼ teaspoon red pepper flakes
2 tablespoons cornstarch
2 tablespoons water

1. Cut peach slices in half with spoon. Place peaches with juice, pork chops, onion, raisins, sugar, vinegar, tapioca, salt, cinnamon and pepper flakes into slow cooker. Cover; cook on LOW 7 to 8 hours.

2. Remove pork to warm platter. Skim off fat from peach mixture. Combine cornstarch and water to make smooth paste. Stir into peach mixture. Cook on HIGH 15 minutes or until sauce is thickened. Adjust seasonings, if desired.

Makes 6 to 8 servings

Ground Cinnamon

Simple Shredded Pork Tacos

2 pounds boneless pork roast
1 cup salsa
1 can (4 ounces) chopped green chilies
½ teaspoon garlic salt
½ teaspoon black pepper

1. Place all ingredients in slow cooker.

2. Cover; cook on LOW 8 hours, or until meat is tender. To serve, use
2 forks to shred pork.   *Makes 6 servings*

Serving Suggestions: Serve with tortillas and your favorite
condiments.

Pork & Tomato Ragout

2 pounds pork stew meat, cut into 1-inch pieces
¼ cup all-purpose flour
3 tablespoons oil
1¼ cups white wine
2 pounds red potatoes, cut into ½-inch pieces
1 can (14½ ounces) diced tomatoes, undrained
1 cup finely chopped onion
1 cup water
½ cup finely chopped celery
2 cloves garlic, minced
½ teaspoon black pepper
1 cinnamon stick
3 tablespoons chopped fresh parsley

1. Toss pork with flour. Heat oil in large skillet over medium-high heat. Add pork to skillet and brown on all sides. Place pork into slow cooker.

2. Add wine to skillet; bring to a boil, scraping up browned bits from bottom of skillet. Pour into slow cooker.

3. Add all remaining ingredients except parsley. Cover; cook on LOW 6 to 8 hours or until pork and potatoes are tender. Remove and discard cinnamon stick. Adjust seasonings, if desired. Sprinkle with parsley just before serving.

Makes 6 servings

Vegetarian Sausage Rice

2 cups chopped green bell peppers
1 can (15½ ounces) dark kidney beans, drained and rinsed
1 can (14½ ounces) diced tomatoes with green bell peppers and
    onions, undrained
1 cup chopped onion
1 cup sliced celery
1 cup water, divided
¾ cup uncooked long-grain white rice
1¼ teaspoons salt
1 teaspoon hot pepper sauce
½ teaspoon dried thyme leaves
½ teaspoon red pepper flakes
3 bay leaves
1 package (8 ounces) vegetable protein breakfast patties,
    thawed
2 tablespoons extra virgin olive oil
½ cup chopped fresh parsley
  Additional hot pepper sauce (optional)

1. Combine bell peppers, beans, tomatoes with juice, onion, celery, ½ cup water, rice, salt, pepper sauce, thyme, pepper flakes and bay leaves in slow cooker. Cover; cook on LOW 4 to 5 hours. Remove and discard bay leaves.

2. Dice breakfast patties. Heat oil in large nonstick skillet over medium-high heat. Add patties; cook 2 minutes or until lightly browned, scraping bottom of skillet occasionally.

3. Place patties in slow cooker. *Do not stir.* Add remaining ½ cup water to skillet; bring to a boil over high heat 1 minute, scraping up bits on bottom of skillet. Add liquid and parsley to slow cooker; stir gently to blend. Serve immediately with additional hot pepper sauce, if desired.   *Makes 8 cups*

South-of-the-Border Macaroni & Cheese

5 cups cooked rotini pasta
2 cups (8 ounces) cubed American cheese
1 can (12 ounces) evaporated milk
1 cup (4 ounces) shredded sharp Cheddar cheese
1 can (4 ounces) diced green chilies, drained
2 teaspoons chili powder
2 medium tomatoes, seeded and chopped
5 green onions, sliced

1. Combine all ingredients, except tomatoes and onions in slow cooker; mix well. Cover; cook on HIGH 2 hours, stirring twice.

2. Stir in tomatoes and green onions; continue cooking until hot.

Makes 4 servings

Vegetable Pasta Sauce

2 cans (14½ ounces each) diced tomatoes, undrained
1 can (14½ ounces) whole tomatoes, undrained
1½ cups sliced mushrooms
1 medium red bell pepper, diced
1 medium green bell pepper, diced
1 small yellow squash, cut into ¼-inch slices
1 small zucchini, cut into ¼-inch slices
1 can (6 ounces) tomato paste
4 green onions, sliced
2 tablespoons dried Italian seasoning
1 tablespoon chopped fresh parsley
3 cloves garlic, minced
1 teaspoon salt
1 teaspoon red pepper flakes (optional)
1 teaspoon black pepper
Hot cooked pasta
Parmesan cheese and fresh basil for garnish (optional)

Good!

Combine all ingredients except pasta and garnishes in slow cooker, stirring until well blended. Cover; cook on LOW 6 to 8 hours. Serve over cooked pasta. Garnish with Parmesan cheese and fresh basil, if desired.

Makes 4 to 6 servings

Three Pepper Pasta Sauce

1 *each* green, red and yellow bell pepper, cut into 1-inch pieces
2 cans (14½ ounces each) diced tomatoes, undrained
1 cup chopped onion
1 can (6 ounces) tomato paste
4 cloves garlic, minced
2 tablespoons olive oil
1 teaspoon dried basil leaves
1 teaspoon dried oregano leaves
½ teaspoon salt
¼ teaspoon red pepper flakes or ground black pepper
    Hot cooked pasta
    Shredded Parmesan or Romano cheese

1. Combine all ingredients except pasta and cheese in slow cooker. Cover; cook on LOW 7 to 8 hours or until vegetables are tender.

2. Adjust seasonings, if desired. Serve with pasta and cheese.

Makes 4 to 6 servings

Tip: 3 cups mixed bell pepper chunks from a salad bar can be substituted for whole peppers.

Vegetarian Lasagna

1 small eggplant, sliced into ½-inch rounds
½ teaspoon salt
2 tablespoons olive oil, divided
1 tablespoon butter
8 ounces mushrooms, sliced
1 small onion, diced
1 can (26 ounces) pasta sauce
1 teaspoon dried basil
1 teaspoon dried oregano
2 cups part-skim ricotta cheese
1½ cups (6 ounces) shredded Monterey Jack cheese
1 cup grated Parmesan cheese, divided
1 package (8 ounces) whole wheat lasagna noodles, cooked and
    drained
1 medium zucchini, thinly sliced

1. Sprinkle eggplant with salt; let sit 10 to 15 minutes. Rinse and pat dry; brush with 1 tablespoon olive oil. Brown on both sides in medium skillet over medium heat. Set aside.

2. Heat remaining 1 tablespoon olive oil and butter in same skillet over medium heat; cook and stir mushrooms and onion until softened. Stir in pasta sauce, basil and oregano. Set aside.

3. Combine ricotta cheese, Monterey Jack cheese and ½ cup Parmesan cheese in medium bowl. Set aside.

4. Spread ⅓ sauce mixture in bottom of slow cooker. Layer with ⅓ lasagna noodles, ½ eggplant, ½ cheese mixture. Repeat layers once. For last layer, use remaining ⅓ of lasagna noodles, zucchini, remaining ⅓ of sauce mixture and top with remaining ½ cup Parmesan.

5. Cover; cook on LOW 6 hours. Let sit 15 to 20 minutes before serving.

Makes 4 to 6 servings

Poached Pears with Raspberry Sauce

4 cups cran-raspberry juice cocktail
2 cups Rhine or Riesling wine
¼ cup sugar
2 cinnamon sticks, broken into halves
4 to 5 firm Bosc or Anjou pears, peeled and cored
1 package (10 ounces) frozen raspberries in syrup, thawed
Fresh berries (optional)

1. Combine juice, wine, sugar and cinnamon stick halves in slow cooker. Submerge pears in mixture. Cover; cook on LOW 3½ to 4 hours or until pears are tender. Remove and discard cinnamon sticks.

2. Process raspberries in food processor or blender until smooth; strain and discard seeds. Spoon raspberry sauce onto serving plates; place pear on top of sauce. Garnish with fresh berries, if desired.

Makes 4 to 5 servings

Peach Cobbler

**2 packages (16 ounces each) frozen peaches, thawed and
    drained**
¾ cup plus 1 tablespoon sugar, divided
2 teaspoons ground cinnamon, divided
½ teaspoon ground nutmeg
¾ cup all-purpose flour
6 tablespoons butter, cut into bits
Whipped cream (optional)

1. Combine peaches, ¾ cup sugar, 1½ teaspoons cinnamon and nutmeg in medium bowl. Place into slow cooker.

2. For topping, combine flour, remaining 1 tablespoon sugar and remaining ½ teaspoon cinnamon in separate bowl. Cut in butter with pastry cutter or 2 knives until mixture resembles coarse crumbs. Sprinkle over peach mixture. Cover; cook on HIGH 2 hours. Serve with freshly whipped cream, if desired. *Makes 4 to 6 servings*

Pineapple Daiquiri Sundae

1 pineapple, cored, peeled, and cut into ½-inch chunks
½ cup dark rum
½ cup sugar
3 tablespoons lime juice
   Peel of 2 limes, cut in long strands
1 tablespoon cornstarch or arrowroot

Place all ingredients in slow cooker; mix well. Cover; cook on HIGH 3 to 4 hours. Serve hot over ice cream, pound cake or shortcakes. Garnish with a few fresh raspberries and mint leaves, if desired.

Makes 4 to 6 servings

Variation: Substitute 1 can (20 ounces) crushed pineapple, drained, for the fresh pineapple. Cook on HIGH 3 hours.

English Bread Pudding

16 slices day-old, firm-textured white bread (1 small loaf)
1¾ cups milk

   1 package (8 ounces) mixed dried fruit, cut into small pieces
  ½ cup chopped nuts
   1 medium apple, cored and chopped
  ⅓ cup packed brown sugar
  ¼ cup butter, melted

   1 egg, lightly beaten
   1 teaspoon ground cinnamon
  ¼ teaspoon ground nutmeg
  ¼ teaspoon ground cloves

Tear bread, with crusts, into 1- to 2-inch pieces. Place in slow cooker. Pour milk over bread; let soak 30 minutes. Stir in dried fruit, nuts and apple. Combine remaining ingredients in small bowl. Pour over bread mixture. Stir well to blend. Cover; cook on LOW 3½ to 4 hours or until skewer inserted in center comes out clean.

Makes 6 to 8 servings

Note: Chopping dried fruits can be difficult. To make the job easier, cut the fruit with kitchen scissors. You can also spray your scissors or chef's knife with nonstick cooking spray before you begin chopping so that the fruit won't stick to the blade.

Chunky Sweet Spiced Apple Butter

4 cups (about 1¼ pounds) peeled, chopped Granny Smith apples
¾ cup packed dark brown sugar
2 tablespoons balsamic vinegar
¼ cup butter, divided
1 tablespoon ground cinnamon
½ teaspoon salt
¼ teaspoon ground cloves
1½ teaspoons vanilla

1. Combine apples, sugar, vinegar, 2 tablespoons butter, cinnamon, salt and cloves in slow cooker. Cover; cook on LOW 8 hours.

2. Stir in remaining 2 tablespoons butter and vanilla. Cool completely.

Makes 2 cups

Serving Suggestions: Serve with roasted meats or on toast.

Triple Delicious Hot Chocolate

⅓ **cup sugar**
¼ **cup unsweetened cocoa powder**
¼ **teaspoon salt**
 3 **cups milk, divided**
¾ **teaspoon vanilla**
 1 **cup heavy cream**
 1 **square (1 ounce) bittersweet chocolate**
 1 **square (1 ounce) white chocolate**
¾ **cup whipped topping**
 6 **teaspoons mini chocolate chips or shaved bittersweet chocolate**

1. Combine sugar, cocoa, salt and ½ cup milk in medium bowl. Beat until smooth. Pour into slow cooker. Add remaining 2½ cups milk and vanilla. Cover; cook on LOW 2 hours.

2. Add cream. Cover and cook on LOW 10 minutes. Stir in bittersweet and white chocolates until melted.

3. Pour hot chocolate into 6 coffee cups. Top each with 2 tablespoons whipped cream and 1 teaspoon chocolate chips.   *Makes 6 servings*

Hot Drinks   45

Mulled Cranberry Tea

2 tea bags
1 cup boiling water
1 bottle (48 ounces) cranberry juice
½ cup dried cranberries (optional)
⅓ cup sugar
1 large lemon, cut into ¼-inch slices
4 cinnamon sticks
6 whole cloves
   Additional thin lemon slices for garnish
   Additional cinnamon sticks for garnish

1. Place tea bags in slow cooker. Pour boiling water over tea bags; cover and let stand 5 minutes. Remove and discard tea bags. Stir in cranberry juice, cranberries, if desired, sugar, lemon slices, 4 cinnamon sticks and cloves. Cover; cook on LOW 2 to 3 hours or on HIGH 1 to 2 hours.

2. Remove and discard lemon slices, cinnamon sticks and cloves. Serve in warm mug with additional fresh lemon slice and cinnamon stick.

Makes 8 servings